SAN FRANCISCO
TRAVEL GUIDE
2023

Discover the Best of San Francisco: A
Comprehensive Guide to Exploring the
City by the Bay

Silva Martin

TABLE OF CONTENTS

INTRODUCTION

San Francisco is a city with a rich and colourful history, stunning natural beauty, and a diverse and innovative culture. Located on the tip of a peninsula in Northern California, the city is renowned for its iconic landmarks, such as the Golden Gate Bridge, Alcatraz Island, and the Painted Ladies.

San Francisco's thriving arts and culture scene, world-class dining, and unique neighbourhoods, including Chinatown and the Haight-Ashbury district, attract millions of visitors each year.

Beyond its cultural offerings, San Francisco is also a centre of innovation, with a vibrant tech industry and numerous startups calling the city home. With its stunning bay views, temperate climate, and endless opportunities for exploration and adventure, San Francisco is a truly unforgettable destination.

CHAPTER 1

Welcome to San Francisco

Welcome to San Francisco, a city that needs no introduction. This vibrant and diverse city located in Northern California offers an array of experiences for visitors.

Firstly, San Francisco is home to some of the world's most iconic landmarks, such as the Golden Gate Bridge, a symbol of American engineering and a marvel of modern architecture. Another must-see attraction is Alcatraz Island, which was once home to one of the world's most notorious prisons and now offers visitors a glimpse into the past through its tours and exhibitions.

Beyond the landmarks, San Francisco is also known for its diverse and unique neighbourhoods. From the historic Chinatown to the colourful Haight-Ashbury district, each neighbourhood offers its own distinct personality and culture.

The city also boasts a thriving arts and culture scene, with world-class museums such as the San Francisco Museum of Modern Art and the de Young Museum, as well as numerous galleries, theatres, and performance venues.

In addition to its cultural offerings, San Francisco is also a food lover's paradise. From the city's famous sourdough bread to its innovative culinary scene, San Francisco has something to offer for every taste and budget.

Finally, the city's natural beauty is another major draw for visitors. The city's mild Mediterranean climate and stunning bay views make it an ideal destination for outdoor activities such as hiking, cycling, and boating.

In summary, San Francisco is a city that offers something for everyone, from its iconic landmarks to its diverse neighbourhoods, thriving arts and culture scene, world-class cuisine, and stunning natural beauty. So come and experience the magic of San Francisco for yourself!

History of San Francisco

The history of San Francisco is rich and fascinating, shaped by a diverse range of cultures and events.

The area where San Francisco is now located was initially home to the Ohlone people, who lived in the region for thousands of years before the arrival of Spanish explorers in the late 18th century. In 1776, Spanish settlers founded a military fort and mission in the area, which eventually grew into the city of San Francisco.

The Gold Rush of 1849 marked a turning point in the city's history, as thousands of people from around the world flocked to San Francisco in search of fortune. The city's population exploded from around 1,000 in 1848 to over 25,000 by 1850, transforming San Francisco into a bustling metropolis.

In the late 19th and early 20th centuries, San Francisco became a hub of innovation and progress. The city played a key role in the development of the transcontinental railroad, and was also home to important cultural movements such as the Beat Generation and the Summer of Love.

Throughout its history, San Francisco has also faced numerous challenges, including devastating earthquakes, fires, and social upheavals. One of the most significant events in the city's history was the 1906 earthquake and subsequent fire, which destroyed much of the city and resulted in the loss of over 3,000 lives.

Today, San Francisco remains a centre of innovation and progress, with a thriving tech industry and a commitment to social and environmental justice. The city's rich history is celebrated through its numerous museums, landmarks, and cultural institutions, which offer visitors a glimpse into the fascinating story of this vibrant and dynamic city.

Why Visit San Francisco in 2023

San Francisco is a city that offers a unique blend of history, culture, innovation, and natural beauty, making it an ideal destination for travellers looking for a truly unforgettable experience. Here are some of the top reasons to visit San Francisco in 2023:

Iconic Landmarks: San Francisco is home to some of the world's most iconic landmarks, such as the Golden

Gate Bridge and Alcatraz Island. These landmarks offer stunning views and a glimpse into the city's rich history and culture.

Diverse Neighbourhoods: San Francisco's diverse neighbourhoods, such as Chinatown, the Mission, and Haight-Ashbury, offer a unique blend of cultures, cuisines, and lifestyles, making them a must-visit for anyone looking to explore the city's vibrant local scene.

Arts and Culture: San Francisco is a cultural hub, with world-class museums, galleries, theatres, and music venues that showcase the city's thriving arts scene.

Innovation and Technology: San Francisco is home to a thriving tech industry, and visitors can explore the city's innovative spirit through its numerous startups, incubators, and co-working spaces.

Outdoor Activities: San Francisco's mild Mediterranean climate and stunning natural beauty make it an ideal destination for outdoor activities such as hiking, cycling, and boating.

Culinary Delights: San Francisco is a food lover's paradise, with a diverse range of cuisines, from traditional sourdough bread to innovative fusion dishes.

Festivals and Events: San Francisco hosts numerous festivals and events throughout the year, from the colourful Pride Parade to the eclectic Outside Lands Music Festival.

In summary, San Francisco is a city that offers something for everyone, from its iconic landmarks and diverse neighbourhoods to its thriving arts and culture scene, innovative spirit, outdoor activities, culinary delights, and exciting festivals and events. So come and experience the magic of San Francisco in 2023!

CHAPTER 2

Planning Your Trip

San Francisco is a vibrant city on the West Coast of the United States, known for its stunning Golden Gate Bridge, eclectic neighbourhoods, and rich cultural heritage. If you're planning a trip to San Francisco, here are some helpful tips to make the most of your visit:

Best time to visit: Spring or fall when the weather is pleasant and the crowds are smaller.

Transportation: Excellent public transportation, bike-friendly, and narrow streets for driving.

Accommodations: Wide range of options from luxury hotels to budget-friendly hostels.

Must-see attractions: Golden Gate Bridge, Alcatraz Island, Fisherman's Wharf, Painted Ladies, and diverse neighbourhoods.

Food and drink: Foodie's paradise with world-class restaurants, coffee shops, and bars. Try the sourdough bread, seafood, and Mission-style burritos.

Outdoor activities: Natural beauty surrounds the city, with options to hike, bike, picnic, or take a whale-watching tour.

Safety: Generally a safe city, but take precautions like avoiding walking alone at night and keeping your valuables close.

By following these tips, you can plan a fun and memorable trip to San Francisco.

Best Time to Visit

San Francisco is a popular tourist destination on the West Coast of the United States, known for its iconic landmarks, diverse neighbourhoods, and vibrant culture. When planning a trip to San Francisco, it's important to consider the best time to visit in order to make the most of your experience.

Here are some quick tips on the best time to visit San Francisco:

Spring (March–May) and fall (September–November) have moderate temperatures and clear skies, making it ideal for outdoor activities and cultural events.

Summer (June–August) can be foggy and chilly, but it's still a popular time for families on vacation.

Winter (December–February) is mild, with fewer tourists, making it a good time to experience holiday festivities.

Overall, the best time to visit San Francisco is during spring or fall when the weather is mild and the crowds are smaller. However, regardless of the season, there are always plenty of things to see and do in this vibrant city.

How to Get to San Francisco Airports:

To reach San Francisco by air, you must choose between two airports: San Francisco International Airport (SFO) or Oakland International Airport (OAK). Book your flight early and check for updates. Make sure you have all necessary travel documents, arrive at the airport early, and be familiar with your airline's baggage policy. When boarding your flight, have your travel documents and boarding pass ready.

Train Stations:

San Francisco has two main train stations: Amtrak's Emeryville Station and Caltrain's San Francisco Station. From Emeryville, you can take a bus or taxi to San Francisco. From Caltrain's San Francisco Station, you can take a taxi, ride-share service, or public transportation to your destination. It's recommended to plan your trip in advance and check the train schedule for any updates or changes. Make sure to have your travel documents and arrive early to avoid any delays.

Bus Stations:

San Francisco has several bus stations, including the Greyhound station and the Transbay Transit Center. From these stations, you can take a taxi, ride-share service, or public transportation to your destination. It's recommended to book your ticket in advance and check the bus schedule for any updates or changes. Make sure to have your travel documents and arrive early to avoid any delays.

Driving:

Driving to San Francisco is an option if you live nearby or want to explore the area by car. San Francisco is well-connected to several major highways, including Highway 101 and Interstate 80. However, be aware that parking in San Francisco can be expensive and traffic can be heavy, especially during peak hours. Plan your route in advance and consider using public transportation or ride-sharing services once you reach your destination to avoid the hassle of parking. It's also recommended to have a GPS or map to navigate the city's streets.

Where to Stay

Hotels:

San Francisco offers a wide range of hotels to fit every budget and travel style. Some popular options include the Hilton San Francisco Union Square, Fairmont San Francisco, and Hotel Nikko San Francisco. These hotels offer a range of amenities, including restaurants, fitness centres, and spa services. Depending on the hotel, room types can range from standard rooms to suites with city views. It's recommended to book your stay in advance, especially during peak travel seasons. Keep in mind that hotel prices can vary greatly depending on location and amenities, so be sure to shop around for the best deal.

Vacation Rentals:
Vacation rentals can be a great option for travellers looking for more space, privacy, and the ability to cook meals. Some popular vacation rental options in San Francisco include Airbnb, Vrbo, and HomeAway. These platforms offer a range of accommodations, from

private rooms to entire apartments or houses. Vacation rentals can be a good choice for families, groups, or long-term stays. However, be aware that some neighbourhoods may have restrictions on short-term rentals, so be sure to check local regulations before booking. It's also recommended to read reviews and communicate with the host before booking to ensure a smooth and comfortable stay.

Hostels:
San Francisco has several affordable hostel options for budget-conscious travellers. Some popular hostels include HI San Francisco Downtown, USA Hostels San Francisco, and Pacific Tradewinds Hostel. These hostels offer

shared dormitory-style rooms, private rooms, and communal spaces for guests to socialise. Some hostels also offer free breakfast, Wi-Fi, and organised activities for guests. It's recommended to book your stay in advance, especially during peak travel seasons. Keep in mind that hostel amenities and room quality can vary, so be sure to read reviews and check the hotel's website for details.

How to Get Around

Public Transportation:

San Francisco has a reliable and convenient public transportation system that includes buses, streetcars, subways, and cable cars. The primary transportation provider is the San Francisco Municipal Transportation Agency (SFMTA), also known as Muni. Muni offers a range of fares, including single-ride tickets and multi-day passes, which can be purchased at vending machines or using the MuniMobile app.

The historic cable cars and streetcars are also popular modes of transportation for tourists. Additionally, the Bay Area Rapid Transit (BART) system provides regional transportation to and from San Francisco. It's recommended to plan your route in advance and check schedules, as some routes may have limited service on weekends or holidays. Keep in mind that public transportation can get crowded during peak hours, so consider travelling during off-peak times if possible.

Taxis and Rideshares:
Taxis and rideshare services like Uber and Lyft are popular options for getting around San Francisco. You can hail a taxi on the street or use an app to request a ride from a rideshare service. The fares for taxis are regulated by the city, while the fares for rideshare services vary based on demand and distance.

Taxis and rideshare services can be a convenient option for getting around the city, especially if you're travelling in a group or need to get somewhere quickly. However, keep in mind that traffic can be heavy in certain areas, so your travel time may vary. It's also important to confirm the pickup location and check the driver's information before getting into the car.

Rental Cars:
Rental cars are available in San Francisco from a variety of car rental companies, including major chains like Hertz, Avis, and Enterprise. Rental cars can be convenient for exploring areas outside of the city, but driving within

San Francisco can be challenging due to heavy traffic, limited parking, and steep hills.

It's recommended to plan your route in advance and familiarise yourself with the city's parking regulations. Keep in mind that parking can be expensive and hard to find in popular areas, so consider using public transportation or rideshares for getting around the city centre. Additionally, tolls may apply when crossing the Golden Gate Bridge or using some highways, so be sure to check for toll roads along your route.

Biking and Walking:

Biking and walking are popular ways to get around in San Francisco due to the city's relatively compact size and bike-friendly infrastructure. There are numerous bike rental shops throughout the city, and many streets have dedicated bike lanes or shared lanes with motorists. Walking can also be a pleasant way to explore the city's unique neighbourhoods and attractions, and many popular destinations are within walking distance of each other.

However, keep in mind that San Francisco's hilly terrain can be challenging for some walkers and cyclists. Additionally, it's important to always obey traffic laws, wear appropriate safety gear, and secure your bike when parked to prevent theft.

Parking:
Parking in San Francisco can be challenging due to limited space and high demand. There are both metered and non-metered street parking options, but availability can vary widely depending on the time of day and location. Parking metres generally accept coins, credit cards, or mobile payments, and time limits and rates vary by neighbourhood.

Some areas also have resident permit parking zones that limit parking to local residents. Additionally, there are many parking garages and lots throughout the city, but prices can be steep, especially in popular tourist areas. It's recommended to research parking options in advance and consider using public transportation or rideshares to avoid the hassle and expense of parking in the city.

CHAPTER 3

Top Things To Do And See In San Francisco

San Francisco, also known as the "City by the Bay," is one of the most vibrant and culturally rich cities in the United States. Here are some top things to do and see in San Francisco:

Golden Gate Bridge: Iconic landmark for a stroll or panoramic views from Baker Beach.

Alcatraz Island: Infamous former prison accessible by ferry for a fascinating history lesson.

Fisherman's Wharf: Touristy area with seafood restaurants and sea lions lounging on the docks.

Chinatown: Authentic cultural experience with traditional shops and delicious food.

Cable Cars: Unique way to see the city by riding up and down the steep hills.

Exploratorium: Hands-on science museum with over 600 interactive exhibits.

Golden Gate Park: Expansive park with hiking, picnicking, and museum visits.

Palace of Fine Arts: Beautiful structure for weddings and photo shoots.

Haight-Ashbury: Colourful neighbourhood associated with the 1960s counterculture movement.

Mission District: Vibrant arts scene, street art, and Mexican cuisine.

Golden Gate Bridge

The Golden Gate Bridge is one of the most iconic landmarks in San Francisco and a must-see attraction for visitors to the city. Spanning 1.7 miles across the Golden Gate Strait, the bridge connects San Francisco to Marin

County and offers stunning views of the bay and the city skyline.

Construction on the bridge began in 1933 and was completed in 1937, at a cost of $35 million. At the time, it was the longest suspension bridge in the world, with two massive towers rising 746 feet above the water.

The bridge is painted in a distinctive shade of International Orange, which was chosen for its visibility in the fog that often rolls in from the Pacific Ocean. The bridge is open to cars, pedestrians, and bicyclists, with separate lanes for each.

Visitors can take a stroll across the bridge on the pedestrian walkway, which offers panoramic views of the bay and the city. The bridge can also be viewed from nearby parks and beaches, such as Crissy Field and Baker Beach.

The Golden Gate Bridge is not only a beloved symbol of San Francisco but also a feat of engineering and an important piece of American history. It has been featured in countless films and TV shows and is a source of inspiration and pride for the city and its residents.

Alcatraz Island

Alcatraz Island, located in San Francisco Bay, is a former federal prison that operated from 1934 to 1963. It was home to some of the country's most notorious criminals, including Al Capone and George "Machine Gun" Kelly. Today, it is a popular tourist attraction, drawing visitors from all over the world.

The prison was built on the rocky island to house federal prisoners who were considered dangerous and difficult to manage. The prison's location on an island in the middle of the bay made it virtually impossible for inmates to escape.

Visitors to Alcatraz can take a ferry from San Francisco to the island, where they can tour the prison and learn about its history. The prison is now a museum, with exhibits and displays that showcase the harsh conditions and daily life inside the prison.

Some of the most popular exhibits include the cell blocks, the dining hall, and the recreation yard. Visitors can also take a guided tour, which includes access to areas of the prison that are not open to the general public.

In addition to its history as a prison, Alcatraz Island is also home to a variety of plants and wildlife, including seabirds and marine mammals. Visitors can explore the island's natural beauty on hiking trails and take in stunning views of the bay and the Golden Gate Bridge.

Overall, Alcatraz Island is a unique and fascinating destination that offers a glimpse into the darker side of American history. It is a must-see attraction for anyone visiting San Francisco.

Fisherman's Wharf

Fisherman's Wharf is a bustling tourist destination in San Francisco that offers a variety of activities, attractions, and dining options. Located on the northern waterfront, the area has a rich history as a fishing port and is still home to a fleet of fishing boats.

Visitors to Fisherman's Wharf can enjoy fresh seafood from a variety of restaurants and food vendors, including crab, clam chowder, and sourdough bread. The area is also home to souvenir shops, museums, and entertainment options such as street performers and live music.

One of the highlights of Fisherman's Wharf is the sea lions that have made their home on the docks. Visitors can watch the sea lions sunbathing and barking as they jockey for position on the floating platforms.

Other popular attractions in the area include the San Francisco Maritime National Historical Park, which includes a collection of historic ships and exhibits on the city's maritime history, and Ripley's Believe It or Not! Museum, which features oddities and curiosities from around the world.

Fisherman's Wharf is also the starting point for boat tours and cruises of the bay, including trips to Alcatraz Island and the Golden Gate Bridge. Visitors can take a leisurely stroll along the waterfront, take in the sights and sounds of the bustling port, and enjoy some of the freshest seafood in the city.

Cable Cars

Cable cars are a unique form of transportation in San Francisco and an iconic symbol of the city. The cable car system was first introduced in the late 19th century as a way to navigate the city's steep hills.

Today, visitors to San Francisco can ride on the city's remaining cable car lines, which are operated by the San Francisco Municipal Transportation Agency (SFMTA). The cable cars run on three lines, with each line offering a different route through the city.

One of the most popular routes is the Powell-Mason line, which runs from

Powell Street to Fisherman's Wharf, offering stunning views of the bay and Alcatraz Island. Another popular route is the Powell-Hyde line, which runs from Powell Street to Lombard Street, known as the "crookedest street in the world."

The cable cars themselves are a historic and charming mode of transportation, with their wooden benches and brass fittings. The cars are powered by cables that run beneath the street, which are pulled by a system of underground motors and wheels.

Riding on a cable car is a unique and memorable experience that offers a glimpse into San Francisco's past.

Visitors can hop on and off at various stops along the route, taking in the city's sights and sounds from a different perspective.

Overall, cable cars are an essential part of San Francisco's identity and a must-try experience for anyone visiting the city.

Chinatown

Chinatown is one of the most vibrant and culturally rich neighbourhoods in San Francisco. It is the oldest and largest Chinatown outside of Asia and is home to a large population of Chinese immigrants and their descendants.

Visitors to Chinatown can explore the neighbourhood's unique architecture, which includes ornate gates, colourful buildings, and narrow alleyways. The streets are lined with shops and restaurants selling traditional Chinese goods and cuisine.

One of the most popular attractions in Chinatown is the Golden Gate Fortune Cookie Factory, where visitors can watch fortune cookies being made by hand and even write their own fortunes to include in the cookies. Another popular attraction is the Chinese Historical Society of America Museum, which offers exhibits and programs that showcase the history and culture of Chinese Americans.

Chinatown is also known for its vibrant festivals and celebrations, including the Chinese New Year Parade, which features elaborate floats, lion dancers, and firecrackers.

Visitors to Chinatown can also explore the neighbourhood's many temples and shrines, including the Tin How Temple and the Buddha's Universal Church.

Overall, Chinatown is a fascinating and vibrant neighbourhood that offers a glimpse into San Francisco's rich cultural diversity. It is a must-see destination for anyone interested in exploring the city's history and culture.

Golden Gate Park

Golden Gate Park is a massive urban park located in San Francisco that spans over 1,000 acres. It is one of the most popular destinations in the city for both tourists and locals alike.

The park offers a variety of attractions and activities for visitors to enjoy. Nature lovers can explore the park's many gardens and green spaces, including the Japanese Tea Garden, the Botanical Garden, and the California Academy of Sciences' Living Roof, which features a mini ecosystem of native California plants.

Art enthusiasts can visit the de Young Museum, which showcases American art from the 17th through the 21st centuries, or the San Francisco Museum of Modern Art, which features contemporary art from around the world.

Sports enthusiasts can take advantage of the park's many athletic facilities, including a golf course, tennis courts, and soccer fields. The park also features a number of playgrounds and picnic areas, making it a great destination for families with children.

One of the most iconic attractions in Golden Gate Park is the Japanese Tea Garden, which features a tranquil pond, a koi fish pond, and a traditional Japanese tea house. Visitors can enjoy a cup of tea and traditional Japanese snacks while taking in the beauty of the garden.

Overall, Golden Gate Park is a must-visit destination in San Francisco that offers something for everyone. Its expansive green spaces, world-class museums, and stunning natural beauty make it a true gem of the city.

Exploratorium

The Exploratorium is a world-renowned science museum located in San Francisco that is dedicated to inspiring curiosity and creativity through hands-on exhibits and interactive experiences.

The museum features more than 650 interactive exhibits that explore a wide range of scientific topics, including physics, biology, psychology, and more. Visitors can experiment with light and colour, test their senses, and even make their own earthquake.

One of the most popular exhibits in the museum is the Tactile Dome, an immersive experience that challenges visitors to navigate a pitch-black maze using only their sense of touch. Other highlights include the outdoor exhibits in the Fisher Bay Observatory Gallery, which offer stunning views of the bay and the Golden Gate Bridge.

The museum also offers a variety of educational programs and workshops for visitors of all ages, including science camps, field trips, and professional development opportunities for educators.

Overall, the Exploratorium is a must-visit destination for anyone interested in science and technology. Its interactive exhibits and engaging programs make it a fun and educational experience for visitors of all ages.

California Palace of the Legion of Honor

The California Palace of the Legion of Honor is a fine arts museum located in San Francisco that features a collection of more than 124,000 works of art from around the world.

The museum's collection includes works from a variety of artistic periods, including ancient art from Egypt, Greece, and Rome, as well as European art from the mediaeval period through the 20th century. The museum is especially known for its collection of European decorative arts, including furniture, ceramics, and glassware.

One of the most iconic exhibits in the museum is the Rodin Gallery, which features a collection of sculptures by the French artist Auguste Rodin. The gallery includes several of Rodin's most famous works, including "The Thinker" and "The Kiss."

The museum is also home to a number of other notable works of art, including paintings by Rembrandt, Rubens, and Monet, as well as ancient artefacts such as mummies and sarcophagi.

In addition to its collection, the California Palace of the Legion of Honor also offers a variety of educational programs and events, including lectures, workshops, and tours.

Overall, the California Palace of the Legion of Honor is a must-visit destination for anyone interested in art and culture. Its impressive collection and beautiful location overlooking the Golden Gate Bridge make it a true gem of San Francisco.

de Young Museum

The de Young Museum is a fine arts museum located in San Francisco's

Golden Gate Park. It is one of the city's most prominent cultural institutions and features a collection of more than 27,000 works of art from around the world.

The museum's collection includes American art from the 17th through the 21st centuries, as well as art from Africa, Oceania, and the Americas. Highlights of the collection include works by Georgia O'Keeffe, Jackson Pollock, and Andy Warhol.

The museum is also known for its stunning architecture, which features a striking copper facade that reflects the colours of the park's surrounding trees. The museum's observation tower offers panoramic views of the park and the city skyline.

In addition to its collection, the de Young Museum also offers a variety of educational programs and events, including lectures, workshops, and family-friendly activities.

Overall, the de Young Museum is a must-visit destination for anyone interested in art and architecture. Its impressive collection and stunning setting make it a true gem of San Francisco.

San Francisco Museum of Modern Art

The San Francisco Museum of Modern Art (SFMOMA) is a world-renowned museum dedicated to modern and contemporary art. Located in the heart of downtown San Francisco, the museum features an extensive collection of more than 33,000 works of art from around the world.

The museum's collection includes works by some of the most famous artists of the 20th and 21st centuries, including Jackson Pollock, Frida Kahlo, and Andy Warhol. The museum also features a number of special exhibitions throughout the year, showcasing the work of contemporary artists from around the world.

SFMOMA is also known for its stunning architecture, which was designed by renowned architect Mario Botta. The museum's distinctive cylindrical building features a grand central atrium and a number of galleries spread across several floors.

In addition to its collection and exhibitions, SFMOMA also offers a variety of educational programs and events, including lectures, workshops, and guided tours.

Overall, SFMOMA is a must-visit destination for anyone interested in modern and contemporary art. Its impressive collection, world-class exhibitions, and stunning architecture make it one of the premier museums of its kind in the world.

The Painted Ladies

The Painted Ladies are a group of Victorian and Edwardian houses located in the Alamo Square neighbourhood of San Francisco. They are famous for their distinctive architectural style, colourful facades, and their appearance in numerous movies and TV shows over the years.

The Painted Ladies consist of six houses in a row, with several other similarly styled houses located nearby.

They were built in the late 19th century and early 20th century and feature ornate details such as gables, turrets, and bay windows.

The houses are particularly striking when viewed from the nearby Alamo Square Park, which provides a beautiful backdrop of downtown San Francisco and the surrounding hills.

The Painted Ladies have become an iconic symbol of San Francisco and are a popular tourist attraction. Visitors can take photos and enjoy the view from the park, or stroll through the neighbourhood to see other examples of Victorian and Edwardian architecture.

Overall, the Painted Ladies are a must-see destination for anyone interested in architecture and history, as well as fans of pop culture who recognize them from their appearances in films and TV shows.

Palace of Fine Arts

The Palace of Fine Arts is a stunning architectural landmark located in San Francisco's Marina District. It was built for the 1915 Panama-Pacific Exposition and is one of the few remaining structures from the event.

The Palace of Fine Arts is designed in the Beaux-Arts style and features a grand rotunda with a dome that rises

162 feet above the ground. The surrounding colonnades are adorned with ornate sculptures and are set against a tranquil lagoon.

Today, the Palace of Fine Arts serves as a popular venue for a variety of cultural events, including art exhibitions, concerts, and weddings. The adjacent Exploratorium museum also provides interactive exhibits that explore the intersection of art, science, and technology.

Visitors to the Palace of Fine Arts can stroll through the grounds and take in the beautiful architecture and scenic surroundings, or attend one of the many events that are hosted there throughout the year.

Overall, the Palace of Fine Arts is a must-see destination for anyone interested in architecture, history, and culture. Its stunning beauty and tranquil setting make it a true gem of San Francisco.

Lombard Street

Lombard Street is a famous street located in the Russian Hill neighbourhood of San Francisco. It is known for its steep, winding road that features eight hairpin turns, making it one of the most crooked streets in the world.

The street was originally designed to make it easier for cars to navigate the steep hill, and the curves were added to slow down traffic and make the road safer for pedestrians.

Today, Lombard Street is a popular tourist attraction, with visitors from all over the world coming to see the unique and picturesque street. Many visitors choose to walk down the street, taking in the stunning views of San Francisco and the Bay Area from the top of the hill.

In addition to its unique design, Lombard Street is also known for its beautiful gardens and landscaping, which line the street and provide a colourful backdrop to the winding road.

Overall, Lombard Street is a must-see destination for anyone visiting San Francisco. Its unique design, stunning views, and beautiful gardens make it a true icon of the city.

Coit Tower

Coit Tower is a historic landmark located on Telegraph Hill in San Francisco. It was built in 1933 and named after Lillie Hitchcock Coit, a prominent San Francisco socialite who left a large sum of money to the city upon her death.

The tower is a 210-foot tall structure that provides panoramic views of San Francisco and the surrounding Bay Area. Visitors can take an elevator to the top of the tower and enjoy the breathtaking views from the observation deck.

The tower is also home to a series of murals that were created by a group of artists during the Great Depression as part of a New Deal program. The murals depict various scenes from San Francisco's history, including its maritime past and its role in the labour movement.

Coit Tower is a popular destination for tourists and locals alike, with many visitors coming to enjoy the views, learn about the city's history through the murals, and take in the beautiful architecture of the tower itself.

Overall, Coit Tower is a must-see destination for anyone visiting San Francisco. Its stunning views and rich history make it a true icon of the city.

Ferry Building Marketplace

The Ferry Building Marketplace is a historic building located on the San Francisco waterfront. Originally built in 1898, the building served as a hub for ferry transportation across the Bay Area.

Today, the Ferry Building Marketplace is a popular destination for locals and tourists alike, with a wide variety of shops, restaurants, and artisanal food vendors. Visitors can sample locally-produced cheeses, charcuterie, and baked goods, or dine at one of the many restaurants that offer cuisine from around the world.

In addition to its food and beverage offerings, the Ferry Building Marketplace is also home to a weekly farmers market that features fresh produce from local farmers and artisans. The farmers market is a great place to sample seasonal produce and learn about sustainable farming practices.

The building itself is also a beautiful example of Beaux-Arts architecture, with a clock tower that rises 245 feet above the ground. Visitors can take a self-guided tour of the building and learn about its history and significance to the city.

Overall, the Ferry Building Marketplace is a must-visit destination for anyone interested in food, architecture, or local history. Its vibrant atmosphere and diverse offerings make it a true gem of San Francisco.

San Francisco Zoo

The San Francisco Zoo is a large urban zoo located in the southwestern corner of San Francisco. It is home to over 1,000 animals from around the world, including tigers, gorillas, penguins, and much more.

One of the zoo's main attractions is the spacious African Savanna exhibit, which features a large grassy plain and a replica of a Kenyan village. Visitors can observe giraffes, zebras, and other African wildlife as they roam freely in a habitat designed to mimic their natural environment.

Another popular exhibit is the Penguin Island, which is home to a colony of African penguins. Visitors can watch these charismatic birds swim and play in their pool or waddle around the exhibit.

The San Francisco Zoo also offers a wide range of educational programs and activities for visitors of all ages. From animal encounters to behind-the-scenes tours, there are plenty of opportunities to learn more about the zoo's animals and conservation efforts.

Overall, the San Francisco Zoo is a great destination for families and animal lovers. Its diverse collection of animals, educational programs, and immersive exhibits make it a unique and memorable experience for visitors of all ages.

AT&T Park

AT&T Park, now known as Oracle Park, is a Major League Baseball stadium located in the South Beach neighbourhood of San Francisco. It is the home of the San Francisco Giants, one of the oldest and most storied teams in professional baseball.

The park opened in 2000 and has since become one of the most iconic stadiums in baseball. Its unique design features a brick exterior, sweeping views of the San Francisco Bay, and a massive Coca-Cola bottle and giant baseball glove as prominent landmarks in the outfield.

In addition to baseball games, AT&T Park is also a popular venue for concerts, festivals, and other events. Its waterfront location and stunning views make it a memorable setting for any occasion.

One of the highlights of a visit to AT&T Park is the food and beverage offerings. The park features a wide variety of local and international cuisine, including classic ballpark fare like hot dogs and nachos, as well as more gourmet options like garlic fries and artisanal pizzas.

Overall, AT&T Park is a must-visit destination for any baseball fan or visitor to San Francisco. Its beautiful setting, unique design, and diverse offerings make it a true gem of the city.

CHAPTER 4

Neighbourhoods of San Francisco

San Francisco has several unique and diverse neighbourhoods, each with its own personality. Some popular ones include the Mission District for food and nightlife, Nob Hill for affluence, Haight-Ashbury for vintage shops, Pacific Heights for stunning views, Chinatown for Chinese culture, and North Beach for Italian cuisine and City Lights Bookstore.

The Mission

The Mission District is one of San Francisco's most vibrant and culturally rich neighbourhoods. It's known for its colourful street art, Latino heritage, and eclectic mix of trendy shops, bars, and restaurants. Visitors to the Mission can explore the historic Mission Dolores, stroll down the vibrant Valencia Street corridor, and indulge in delicious Mexican cuisine.

The neighbourhood is also home to several parks and green spaces, including the popular Mission Dolores Park. At night, the Mission comes alive with a lively nightlife scene that includes everything from dive bars to dance clubs. Whether you're a foodie, art lover, or just looking for a fun night out, the Mission is a must-visit destination in San Francisco.

Haight-Ashbury

Haight-Ashbury is an iconic neighbourhood in San Francisco that is famous for its association with the 1960s counterculture movement. Today, it's a mix of vintage shops, funky boutiques, and colourful Victorian homes. Visitors to Haight-Ashbury can explore the neighbourhood's historic sites, including the former homes of famous musicians like Janis Joplin and the Grateful Dead.

The neighbourhood is also home to several beautiful parks, including the stunning Golden Gate Park. In addition to its rich cultural history,

Haight-Ashbury is a great destination for shopping, dining, and nightlife. Whether you're interested in vintage clothing, live music, or delicious food, Haight-Ashbury has something for everyone.

Castro

Castro is a vibrant and historic neighbourhood in San Francisco that is known for its LGBTQ community and activism. Visitors to Castro can explore the neighbourhood's colourful streets, filled with rainbow flags and historical landmarks like the Castro Theatre. The neighbourhood is also home to several shops, bars, and restaurants that cater to the LGBTQ community, including the iconic Twin Peaks Tavern.

In addition to its rich cultural history, Castro is a great destination for nightlife and entertainment, with several bars and nightclubs offering a lively and welcoming atmosphere. Whether you're looking to learn about LGBTQ history, enjoy a night out, or simply soak up the neighbourhood's unique atmosphere, Castro is a must-visit destination in San Francisco.

Pacific Heights

Pacific Heights is one of San Francisco's most affluent neighbourhoods and is known for its stunning views of the Bay, Victorian architecture, and upscale shops and restaurants. Visitors to Pacific Heights can stroll through the neighbourhood's picturesque streets, lined with grand mansions and charming row houses. The neighbourhood is also home to several popular attractions, including the historic Haas-Lilienthal House and the popular Fillmore Street shopping district.

In addition to its luxury shopping and dining, Pacific Heights offers several beautiful parks and green spaces, including Lafayette Park and Alta Plaza Park. Whether you're looking for high-end shopping and dining or just want to enjoy some of the city's most beautiful architecture and views, Pacific Heights is a must-visit destination in San Francisco.

Nob Hill

Nob Hill is a luxurious and affluent neighbourhood in San Francisco that offers stunning views of the city and a rich history. Visitors to Nob Hill can explore the neighbourhood's grand mansions, luxury hotels, and historic landmarks like the Grace Cathedral. The neighbourhood is also a popular destination for upscale shopping and dining, with several high-end boutiques and restaurants located along its picturesque streets.

In addition to its luxurious offerings, Nob Hill is also home to several beautiful parks and green spaces, including Huntington Park and the historic Cable Car Museum. Whether you're looking for a taste of luxury or simply want to enjoy some of the city's most beautiful architecture and views, Nob Hill is a must-visit destination in San Francisco.

North Beach

North Beach is a charming and lively neighbourhood in San Francisco that is known for its rich Italian heritage and delicious cuisine. Visitors to North Beach can explore the neighbourhood's picturesque streets, lined with colourful cafes, bakeries, and restaurants serving up authentic Italian dishes. The neighbourhood is also home to several popular attractions, including the iconic City Lights Bookstore and the historic Saints Peter and Paul Church.

In addition to its Italian culture, North Beach offers several beautiful parks and green spaces, including the popular Washington Square Park. At night, the neighbourhood comes alive with a vibrant nightlife scene that includes everything from cosy bars to dance clubs. Whether you're looking to indulge in delicious food, explore the city's literary history, or enjoy a fun night out, North Beach is a must-visit destination in San Francisco.

Russian Hill

Russian Hill is a picturesque and charming neighbourhood in San Francisco that offers stunning views of the city and a unique blend of history and modernity. Visitors to Russian Hill can explore the neighbourhood's steep and winding streets, lined with beautiful Victorian homes and trendy boutiques. The neighbourhood is also home to several popular attractions, including the iconic Lombard Street, the historic Cable Car Museum, and the picturesque Macondray Lane.

In addition to its beautiful architecture and attractions, Russian Hill offers several beautiful parks and green spaces, including the popular Alice Marble Park. Whether you're looking for a taste of history, stunning views of the city, or simply want to enjoy some of the city's most beautiful architecture and parks, Russian Hill is a must-visit destination in San Francisco.

Presidio

Presidio is a scenic and historic park in San Francisco that offers beautiful views of the Golden Gate Bridge and a unique blend of natural beauty and history. Visitors to Presidio can explore the park's stunning landscapes, which include hiking trails, beaches, and several scenic overlooks. The park is also home to several historic landmarks, including the famous Palace of Fine Arts and the historic Presidio Officers' Club.

In addition to its natural beauty and history, Presidio offers several cultural attractions, including the Walt Disney Family Museum and the Yoda Statue. Whether you're looking to explore the city's natural beauty, learn about its history, or simply enjoy a day outdoors, Presidio is a must-visit destination in San Francisco.

Japantown

Japantown is a vibrant and cultural neighbourhood in San Francisco that is known for its unique blend of Japanese and American culture. Visitors to Japantown can explore the neighbourhood's picturesque streets, filled with shops, restaurants, and markets selling everything from traditional Japanese goods to modern fashions.

The neighbourhood is also home to several popular attractions, including the Japan Center mall, the Kabuki Springs & Spa, and the historic Peace Pagoda. In addition to its cultural offerings, Japantown hosts several festivals and events throughout the year, including the Cherry Blossom Festival and the Nihonmachi Street Fair. Whether you're looking to immerse yourself in Japanese culture, enjoy delicious food, or simply soak up the neighbourhood's unique atmosphere, Japantown is a must-visit destination in San Francisco.

Marina District

Marina District is a picturesque and trendy neighbourhood in San Francisco that offers stunning views of the Golden Gate Bridge and a lively atmosphere. Visitors to Marina District can explore the neighbourhood's picturesque streets, lined with trendy shops, restaurants, and cafes. The neighbourhood is also home to several popular attractions, including the Palace of Fine Arts, the Exploratorium, and the Fort Mason Center for Arts & Culture.

In addition to its cultural offerings, Marina District offers several beautiful parks and green spaces, including the popular Marina Green and Crissy Field. At night, the neighbourhood comes alive with a vibrant nightlife scene that includes everything from rooftop bars to trendy clubs. Whether you're looking for a taste of the city's trendiest offerings, stunning views of the Golden Gate Bridge, or simply want to enjoy some of the city's most beautiful parks and green spaces, Marina District is a must-visit destination in San Francisco.

Inner Sunset

Inner Sunset is a charming and laid-back neighbourhood in San Francisco that offers a unique blend of natural beauty and urban charm. Visitors to Inner Sunset can explore the neighbourhood's cosy streets, lined with cute boutiques, coffee shops, and restaurants serving up delicious cuisine from around the world. The neighbourhood is also home to several popular attractions, including the Golden Gate Park, the San Francisco Botanical Garden, and the de Young Museum. In addition to its cultural offerings, Inner Sunset offers several beautiful parks and green spaces, including the popular Sunset Reservoir and Grand View Park. Whether you're looking to enjoy a day outdoors, explore the city's cultural offerings, or simply soak up the neighbourhood's laid-back atmosphere, Inner Sunset is a must-visit destination in San Francisco.

CHAPTER 5

Outdoor Activities In San Francisco

San Francisco offers a variety of outdoor activities, including Golden Gate Park, Alcatraz Island, Fisherman's Wharf, the Golden Gate Bridge, Lands End, Presidio Park, Baker Beach, and Muir Woods.

Hiking

Lands End:

Hiking at Lands End is a popular activity for locals and tourists in San Francisco. The 3.4-mile round-trip trail offers breathtaking views of the Golden Gate Bridge and the Pacific Ocean. The trail is relatively easy and accessible for hikers of all levels, with options for shorter or longer hikes. Along the way, you can explore the ruins of the Sutro Baths, visit the historic Point Lobos Lighthouse, and spot wildlife such as sea lions and birds. Be sure to wear comfortable shoes and dress in layers, as the weather can be unpredictable. Parking can be limited, so arrive early or consider taking public transportation.

Mount Tamalpais:
Mount Tamalpais offers some of the best hiking opportunities in the San Francisco Bay Area. With over 60 miles of trails, hikers can choose from a variety of routes with stunning views of the Bay, the Pacific Ocean, and the

surrounding hillsides. The Dipsea Trail is a popular choice, a 7.4-mile trail that takes hikers from Mill Valley to Stinson Beach.

The Steep Ravine Trail is another great option, with waterfalls, lush forests, and stunning views of the coastline. Hikers can also climb to the top of Mount Tamalpais for panoramic views of the Bay Area. Visitors should be prepared for changing weather conditions and steep terrain, and bring plenty of water and snacks. A parking fee is required at most trailheads.

Muir Woods:
Hiking in Muir Woods is a unique experience, as it offers visitors the

chance to walk among towering redwood trees that are over 1,000 years old. The park offers several hiking trails, ranging from easy strolls to more challenging hikes. The most popular trail is the 1.5-mile loop through the main grove, which takes visitors past some of the park's most iconic trees.

For a longer hike, visitors can take the 4-mile Dipsea Trail from Muir Woods to Stinson Beach. Due to the popularity of the park, reservations are required to enter and park in Muir Woods, and it's recommended to make them in advance. Visitors should wear comfortable shoes and dress in layers, as the park can be cool and damp even on warm days.

Beaches

Baker Beach:

Baker Beach is a beautiful sandy beach in San Francisco with stunning views of the Golden Gate Bridge. The beach is a popular spot for sunbathing, picnics, and swimming, although the water can be cold and the waves can be strong.

Hiking trails along the coastal bluffs offer breathtaking views of the ocean and the bridge. The northern end of the beach is clothing-optional, while the southern end is family-friendly. Visitors should be aware that the currents and undertow can be dangerous, and there are no lifeguards on duty. Parking can be limited, so arrive early or consider taking public transportation.

Ocean Beach:
Ocean Beach is a long stretch of sandy beach along the western edge of San Francisco, bordering the Pacific Ocean. The beach is known for its strong waves and currents, making it a popular spot for experienced surfers and swimmers. However, visitors should be cautious and aware of the dangers of the ocean.

The beach is also a great spot for walking, picnicking, and watching the sunset. The nearby Cliff House offers a restaurant and observation deck with panoramic views of the ocean. Visitors should dress warmly, as the beach can be windy and cool even on warm days. Parking can be limited, so arrive early or consider taking public transportation.

Crissy Field:
Crissy Field is a beautiful beach in San Francisco that offers stunning views of the Golden Gate Bridge and the Bay. The beach is popular for its wide sandy shorelines, grassy fields, and picnic areas. Visitors can also rent bikes, rollerblades, or kayaks to explore the nearby paths and waterways. Crissy Field is a great spot for families, dog

walkers, and anyone looking to enjoy the outdoors. Visitors should be aware that the water can be cold and currents can be strong, so swimming is not recommended. Parking can be limited, so arrive early or consider taking public transportation.

Biking

Golden Gate Park:

Biking through Golden Gate Park is a popular activity for locals and tourists in San Francisco. The park offers several miles of bike-friendly paths that wind through gardens, lakes, and museums. Visitors can rent bikes from several vendors located near the park, or bring their own bikes. Some popular destinations to visit while biking in the park include the Japanese Tea Garden, the De Young Museum, and the Conservatory of Flowers. The park also has several picnic areas and restrooms for visitors. Visitors should be aware of other park users, and follow traffic rules and signs. Helmets are strongly recommended.

Embarcadero:
Biking along the Embarcadero is a great way to explore San Francisco's waterfront. The bike path follows the eastern edge of the city, offering views of the Bay Bridge, the Ferry Building, and the Bay. Bikes can be rented from several vendors located near the Embarcadero, or visitors can bring

their own bikes. The path is flat and easy to navigate, making it a great option for bikers of all levels. Some popular destinations to visit while biking along the Embarcadero include Fisherman's Wharf, Pier 39, and AT&T Park. Visitors should be aware of other pedestrians and cyclists, and follow traffic rules and signs. Helmets are strongly recommended.

Bay Trail:
Biking the Bay Trail is a unique way to experience the San Francisco Bay Area, offering scenic views of the Bay and the surrounding hills. The trail covers over 500 miles of paths and bike lanes, with access points throughout the region. Bikers can ride past historic

landmarks, wetlands, and wildlife habitats, with several parks and picnic areas along the way. The Bay Trail is mostly flat and easy to navigate, making it a great option for bikers of all levels. Some popular sections of the trail include the Richmond-San Rafael Bridge, the San Francisco Bay Bridge, and the San Mateo Bridge. Visitors should be aware of other trail users, and follow traffic rules and signs. Helmets are strongly recommended.

Kayaking

San Francisco Bay:

Kayaking in the San Francisco Bay is an exciting way to explore the city's waterfront and get up close to iconic landmarks such as the Golden Gate Bridge and Alcatraz Island. Several kayak rental companies offer guided tours and kayak rentals, with options for both beginners and experienced kayakers.

Visitors can paddle around the piers and marinas, or venture out to the Bay to see the sights from a unique perspective. Kayaking in the Bay can be challenging, with strong currents and changing weather conditions, so visitors should be prepared and follow safety guidelines. Paddleboarding is also a popular option for exploring the Bay.

Tomales Bay:

Kayaking on Tomales Bay is a popular activity for nature enthusiasts and outdoor adventurers in the San Francisco Bay Area. Tomales Bay is located in Point Reyes National Seashore, offering pristine waters, secluded beaches, and stunning views of the surrounding mountains. Visitors can rent kayaks from several outfitters located in the area, or bring their own kayaks.

The calm waters of the bay make it a great spot for kayaking, with options for both beginners and experienced kayakers. Some popular destinations to visit while kayaking on Tomales Bay include Hog Island, Heart's Desire

Beach, and Marshall Beach. Visitors should be aware of changing weather conditions, and follow safety guidelines, including wearing a lifejacket and avoiding areas with strong currents.

CHAPTER 6

Food And Drink In San Francisco

San Francisco's food and drink scene is diverse and vibrant, featuring local favourites like clam chowder and Mission-style burritos, as well as artisanal cocktails, craft beers, and wines. The city is known for c food festivals, farmers' markets, and proximity to Napa Valley and Sonoma wineries.

Best Restaurant

Fine Dining:

San Francisco is home to several outstanding fine dining restaurants that offer exceptional cuisine, elegant atmospheres, and impeccable service. The French Laundry, Quince, Atelier Crenn, and Benu are among the city's most acclaimed restaurants, offering unique culinary experiences that attract foodies from around the world.

Casual Dining:
San Francisco's casual dining scene offers a variety of great restaurants with a laid-back atmosphere and a focus on quality food and service. Tartine Manufactory, Burma Love, Nopa, and Souvla are among the city's best casual dining options, offering a range of delicious and satisfying dishes.

Ethnic Cuisine:

San Francisco has a diverse and vibrant ethnic cuisine scene with outstanding restaurants that offer authentic and flavorful dishes. Zuni Cafe and Saison are among the city's most acclaimed restaurants for Mediterranean and Japanese-inspired cuisine, respectively. Other notable restaurants include Burma Superstar for Burmese cuisine, La Ciccia for Sardinian dishes, and Yank Sing for Cantonese specialties.

Farmers' Markets

Ferry Plaza Farmers Market:

The Ferry Plaza Farmers Market is a popular farmers' market in San Francisco, located on the waterfront. It features over 100 vendors offering a diverse selection of local and seasonal produce, meats, seafood, and artisanal foods. In addition to food, the market hosts events and classes on cooking, gardening, and sustainable agriculture, making it a hub for the local food community. The market is a must-visit destination for foodies and those looking to experience San Francisco's local food scene.

Alemany Farmers' Market:
The Alemany Farmers' Market in San Francisco is an old and beloved market located in the Bernal Heights neighbourhood. It is open year-round on Saturdays and features a diverse selection of vendors offering fresh

produce, meats, and artisanal foods. The market is known for its affordable prices and welcoming community atmosphere, making it a popular destination for locals and visitors alike.

Craft Breweries

Anchor Brewing Company:
Anchor Brewing Company is an iconic craft brewery in San Francisco that has been in operation since 1896. It offers a range of year-round and seasonal beers, including its famous Anchor Steam Beer. Visitors can take tours of the brewery and enjoy tastings in the taproom. The brewery is also committed to sustainable brewing practices. It is a must-visit destination for beer enthusiasts and those

interested in the history of American craft beer.

Speakeasy Ales & Lagers:
Speakeasy Ales & Lagers is a popular craft brewery in San Francisco known for its bold and flavorful beers, such as Big Daddy IPA and Prohibition Ale. Visitors can enjoy tastings and brewery tours, and the brewery also hosts events and food trucks. It's a fun destination for beer lovers in a lively atmosphere.

21st Amendment Brewery:
21st Amendment Brewery is a renowned craft brewery in San Francisco with two locations. It offers a variety of year-round and seasonal

beers, including its flagship Hell or High Watermelon and Brew Free or Die IPA. Visitors can enjoy tastings and tours, and the brewery also features a full kitchen serving delicious food. It's a great destination for beer enthusiasts and foodies alike.

Wineries

Napa Valley:

Napa Valley is a world-famous wine region just north of San Francisco, with over 400 wineries producing some of the finest wines in the world. Visitors can explore the wineries and vineyards, and enjoy tastings and tours. The valley also offers a range of culinary experiences, making it a must-visit destination for wine lovers and foodies alike.

Sonoma County:

Sonoma County is a renowned wine region located west of Napa Valley, with over 425 wineries. Visitors can explore the wineries and vineyards, enjoy tastings and tours, and indulge in a range of culinary experiences. Sonoma County is a must-visit destination for wine lovers and those seeking a relaxing wine country experience.

CHAPTER 7

Day Trips From San Francisco

San Francisco offers great day trip options, including Muir Woods, Napa Valley, Monterey and Carmel-by-the-Sea, Silicon Valley, and Point Reyes National Seashore. These destinations are all within a 2-hour drive, providing visitors with the opportunity to explore the region's natural beauty, world-renowned wine region, technology, and coastal towns.

Wine Country

Napa Valley:

Napa Valley's Wine Country is a paradise for wine lovers, offering over

400 wineries to taste from, unique vineyard tours, scenic train rides, and a diverse culinary scene. Outdoor activities like hot air balloon rides, hiking, and cycling also provide a chance to explore the valley's stunning beauty.

Sonoma County:
Sonoma County's Wine Country is a beautiful region with over 425 wineries, picturesque landscapes, and a diverse culinary scene. Outdoor activities like kayaking, biking, and hiking provide a chance to explore the area's natural beauty. The region is also committed to sustainable winemaking practices, making it a

must-visit for anyone travelling to Northern California.

Muir Woods

Muir Woods is a National Monument near San Francisco famous for its old-growth coastal redwood forest. The park offers hiking trails for all skill levels, ranger programs, and a chance to see wildlife. The wheelchair-accessible boardwalk and audio tours make it accessible to all visitors. Muir Woods is an excellent destination for nature lovers and a great escape from the city.

Half Moon Bay

Half Moon Bay is a picturesque coastal town just south of San Francisco. It offers stunning beaches, nature trails, and a diverse culinary scene. Festivals like the Half Moon Bay Art and Pumpkin Festival are popular, and outdoor activities such as fishing, kayaking, horseback riding, and golfing are available. Half Moon Bay is perfect for a day trip or weekend getaway from San Francisco.

Santa Cruz

Santa Cruz is a coastal city south of San Francisco known for its beaches, surfing, redwood forests, diverse dining, and vibrant arts and culture scene. The Santa Cruz Beach Boardwalk and Natural Bridges State Beach are popular attractions, and Henry Cowell Redwoods State Park offers hiking and camping. Santa Cruz also has a diverse culinary scene and many galleries, theatres, and live music venues. It's a great destination for a day trip or weekend getaway from San Francisco.

Monterey and Carmel

Monterey and Carmel are charming coastal towns south of San Francisco. Cannery Row and the Monterey Bay Aquarium are popular attractions in Monterey, while the 17-Mile Drive and Point Lobos State Reserve offer scenic views. Carmel is a picturesque town known for its cottages, galleries, and shops, and is home to the famous Mission San Carlos Borromeo del Rio Carmelo. Both towns offer excellent seafood, farm-to-table cuisine, and international flavours. Monterey and Carmel are perfect for a day trip or weekend getaway from San Francisco.

Lake Tahoe

Lake Tahoe is a breathtaking freshwater lake in the Sierra Nevada mountains, about a three-hour drive from San Francisco. It offers endless outdoor activities, such as hiking, biking, skiing, snowboarding, and water sports. Lake Tahoe also has a vibrant dining and entertainment scene, with excellent restaurants, bars, and casinos.

The area has many accommodation options, including hotels, resorts, cabins, and vacation rentals. Lake Tahoe is a must-visit destination for anyone seeking stunning scenery and a relaxing escape from San Francisco.

CHAPTER 8

PRACTICAL INFORMATION FOR TRAVELLERS

Visa Requirements:

Travellers to San Francisco should check visa requirements before their trip. Some countries are eligible for the Visa Waiver Program (VWP), allowing a 90-day visit without a visa. Others must apply for a B-1 or B-2 visa. Electronic System for Travel Authorization (ESTA) is required for VWP. Entry is not guaranteed, and Customs and Border Protection (CBP) officers have the final decision. Check the U.S. Department of State website for up-to-date information.

Currency and Exchange Rates:

In San Francisco, the currency used is the U.S. dollar (USD), which is widely accepted. Foreign currency exchange services are available but can have varying rates and fees. Many merchants accept credit cards, but check for foreign transaction fees. Plan to bring USD and use credit cards where possible.

Safety and Security:

While San Francisco is generally safe, travellers should take precautions to avoid property crimes and stay in well-lit areas. Wear sturdy shoes to navigate the city's varied terrain and have emergency contact numbers on hand. With proper precautions, San Francisco is a safe destination.

Health and Medical Care:
San Francisco has numerous healthcare options, but medical care can be expensive in the United States. Travellers should have adequate medical insurance coverage and take precautions to stay healthy, such as practising good hygiene and protecting themselves from the sun. San Francisco also offers alternative medicine options, such as acupuncture and yoga.

Language and Communication:
English is the main language spoken in San Francisco, but other languages are

also spoken. Basic knowledge of English phrases is helpful, and translation services are often available. San Francisco is a diverse and inclusive city, so it's important to be respectful of different cultures and customs.

Tips for Solo Travelers:
Solo travel in San Francisco can be enjoyable with proper planning and precautions. Stay in a central and safe location, be aware of your surroundings, and consider joining group activities. Use the public transportation system and plan your itinerary but leave room for spontaneity. Stay connected with loved ones and trust your instincts.

Tips for Budget Travelers:

Budget travel in San Francisco is possible with these tips: travel during the off-season, use public transportation, look for budget accommodations, enjoy free attractions, find discounts on activities, eat at affordable restaurants, and shop at local markets and thrift stores.

CONCLUSION

Final Thoughts

San Francisco is a unique and vibrant city, offering a range of experiences for travellers. From the iconic Golden Gate Bridge to the historic cable cars, there is no shortage of things to see and do. The city's diverse culture, world-class cuisine, and stunning natural beauty make it a must-visit destination.

However, San Francisco can also present some challenges for travellers, such as high costs and traffic congestion. With proper planning and research, these challenges can be mitigated, and travellers can have a rewarding and enjoyable trip.

Overall, San Francisco is a city that truly has something for everyone, and it's worth exploring all that it has to offer.

Resources for Further Information

For travellers looking for more information on San Francisco, there are a variety of resources available. The San Francisco Travel Association website provides detailed information on attractions, accommodations, and events in the city. The San Francisco Chronicle newspaper also offers comprehensive coverage of local news and events.

Additionally, online travel forums such as TripAdvisor and Lonely Planet can provide valuable insights and recommendations from fellow travellers. Guidebooks, such as the Lonely Planet San Francisco guide, can also offer detailed information and suggestions for exploring the city.

Overall, there are many resources available for travellers to learn more about San Francisco and plan their trip to this exciting and dynamic city.

Acknowledgments and Credits

In conclusion, we would like to acknowledge the contribution of Silva

Martin for providing insights and expertise on San Francisco as a travel destination. We are grateful for her knowledge and expertise, which helped to inform this guide.

We also acknowledge the various sources that provided information for this guide, including the San Francisco Travel Association, the San Francisco Chronicle, and online travel forums such as TripAdvisor and Lonely Planet. Additionally, we recognize the contribution of guidebooks, such as the Lonely Planet San Francisco guide.

We hope that this guide, with Silva Martin's contribution, has been informative and helpful for travellers planning a trip to San Francisco.

Made in the USA
Monee, IL
12 November 2023

46388109R00079